Original title:
Tropical Awakening

Copyright © 2025 Creative Arts Management OÜ
All rights reserved.

Author: Nash Everly
ISBN HARDBACK: 978-1-80581-558-7
ISBN PAPERBACK: 978-1-80581-085-8
ISBN EBOOK: 978-1-80581-558-7

Island Whispers

Coconut crabs do the cha-cha,
As palm trees giggle in the breeze.
Laughter bubbles in the warm sun,
While parrots squawk, 'Oh, just tease!'

Flip-flops dancing on the sand,
Seagulls join in with a screech.
Pineapple hats on every head,
As waves declare, 'Oh, let's preach!'

Dawn of the Emerald Paradise

Sunrise brings a funky beat,
Birds wear shades to greet the dawn.
Monkeys play jazz on the tree tops,
While iguanas give a yawn.

Lime-green waves begin to sway,
Crabs wear bling, oh what a sight!
Fish parade in sparkly shoes,
As morning brews in pure delight!

Lush Dreams in the Sunlight

The mango tree stands like a boss,
With sticky juice for all to share.
Bees buzz in a conga line,
While lizards flash their vibrant flair.

Hammocks sway as giggles burst,
Kids splashing in the glimmering sea.
A snail's race, oh what a fuss,
In this land of glee and spree!

Secrets of the Vibrant Grove

In a grove where laughter blooms,
A mystery of coconuts unfolds.
Geckos in tuxedos prance,
As jellyfish weave tales untold.

Frogs croak symphonies at dusk,
While fireflies dance on a whim.
Each petal whispers secrets loud,
In this garden's joyous hymn!

Rejuvenation in the Warmth of Paradise

Sunshine tickles the palm tree's face,
Chasing away the sleepy embrace.
Coconuts dance to a silly tune,
While crabs waltz beneath the bright moon.

Laughter echoes in colorful bars,
As flamingos gossip with the stars.
Flip-flops flop as we twirl with glee,
Those palm drinks promise a wild spree.

Sandy beards and sunburned cheers,
We toast to friendship and vibrant years.
A parrot squawks with mischief in mind,
As we lose our thoughts, leaving cares behind.

The breeze sends secrets on a spree,
A fish jumps up and pranks a bee.
What bliss is found in jungle jive,
Where even the sloths seem to come alive!

Cascade of the Tropical Rain

Raindrops tumble in a playful slide,
Little puddles become a joyous ride.
Kids with paper boats, laughter galore,
Splashing through waters, they dance and soar.

Umbrellas flip in an ironic twist,
As ducks join in on the rainy list.
Clouds are grumpy, yet who can complain?
The sunshine awaits, with no hint of pain.

Misty streams and joyful romps,
Chasing rainbows from lily to swamps.
The world is brighter when drenched in cheer,
Even the frogs have a croaky leer.

Wet hair jokes and giggles abound,
With every drop, more silliness found.
Rain showers bring the best of delight,
Connecting us all in nature's light!

A Symphony of Entwined Vines

Vines twist and twirl with nimble grace,
As monkeys swing in this leafy space.
Laughter erupts from the treetop bands,
Where each furry friend shares his plans.

Colors crash like a painter's dream,
Fruits burst forth in a juicy stream.
A snail joins a dance, though quite slow,
While toucans cheer with a colorful show.

Grapes gossip as they dangle near,
Stories of wind and sun they share clear.
A lizard croons with a comical flair,
Demanding praises for his bright green hair.

Each leaf hums with a vibrant voice,
Nature's rhythm makes us rejoice.
In this jungle party, we unwindingly sway,
Finding joy in the wild, come what may!

Reawakening the Still Waters

Napping waters wake with a funny splash,
Where turtles plot their slow-motion dash.
Frogs croak a tune with comedic flair,
Dancing on lily pads, they make us stare.

Fish do flips, showing off their prance,
While dragonflies join in the playful dance.
A moody heron tries to impress,
With wobbly legs, it's a clumsy mess.

Reflections ripple with giggles and cheer,
Even the reeds lend a floppy ear.
A hippo's snore bubbles up from below,
In this serene pool, we find the flow.

Chasing the sunlight, a breeze starts to tease,
Tickling the waters, it stirs with ease.
In this quiet haven, laughter takes flight,
Awakening beauty, oh what a sight!

Life at the Waters' Edge

Sandy toes and salty hair,
Crabs scuttle past without a care.
Someone's hat flies off the head,
A seagull snatches it instead!

Footprints play a hide-and-seek,
Laughter echoes, cheek to cheek.
A napkin sails on breezy flight,
Picnic plans, now out of sight!

Resplendent Flowers in the Breeze

Petals dance like clowns in bloom,
Bees buzzing loud, they bring the boom.
A butterfly's laugh echoes so bright,
He trips on pollen—what a sight!

Colors fight for who'll be seen,
A gardener winks with a grin, so keen.
Tulips blush in hues of jest,
Roses boast, but who's the best?

Solstice in the Tropics

Sunscreen mixed with laughter's breeze,
Flip-flops squeak like giddy bees.
The sun's a prankster, up so high,
It plays peekaboo in the sky!

A hammock sways, a playful threat,
To take your nap, but here you fret.
As night creeps in, the crickets sway,
Who knew that they could dance this way?

Drifting on the Gentle Waves

Floats are flying like a kite,
Rubber ducks causing a great fright!
A wave comes crashing, splashes fun,
Chasing sunbeams, oh what a run!

Seashells chatter like old friends,
The ocean plays its silly bends.
Caught in seaweed, what a tease,
Just a floaty, aiming to please!

The Secret Life of Tropical Gardens

Underneath the leafy greens,
The garden gnomes hold debates,
Arguing over whose plants sprout,
While the snails set up their fates.

A parrot flirts with passing bees,
Telling jokes that make them buzz,
While a lazy lizard lounges on,
And dreams of tasty garden fuzz.

The flowers wear their brightest hues,
Competing for the most attention,
A toucan swoops with silly flaps,
Prompting laughter in the pension.

In shadows, where the critters scheme,
A hedgehog draws a silly map,
Charting routes to berry treats,
While alligators take a nap.

A Canvas of Colorful Ferns

Ferns in patterns twist and twine,
Wearing hats of morning dew,
They gossip in the lightened breeze,
About a squirrel with a shoe.

Green fronds whisper silly tales,
Of how they love the sun's embrace,
While flowers dance a wiggly jig,
As butterflies join the race.

A chameleon changes color fast,
To match a rather loud piñata,
The ferns all laugh, a merry crew,
Who think they need a banana.

Underneath the vibrant sky,
Lizards strut with utmost flair,
Winking at the ladybugs,
As if they really care!

Melody of the Ocean's Caress

The waves roll in with playful sounds,
Tickling shores with seafoam lace,
While crabs do a silly sideways dance,
Celebrating their ocean base.

A dolphin pops up to say hi,
Wearing sunglasses, looking cool,
While seagulls squawk their morning news,
And the jellyfish try to rule.

Surfboards line the sandy shore,
With goofy messages in the sand,
Each wave a chance to surf and fall,
A constant game that's always grand.

The tide rolls back with laughter loud,
As fish leap up in sudden cheer,
The ocean hums its funny tune,
An anthem for all to hear!

The Promise of Sun and Water

Sunshine peeks through leafy tops,
Promising a brighter day,
While rain clouds rumble all around,
In a most dramatic way.

The flowers stretch, they yawn and sway,
As droplets tap and dance along,
Each petal soaked in nature's fun,
A colorful, fragrant song.

Puddles form for small frogs' games,
Who leap and splash with joyful glee,
While others strut like tiny kings,
In a realm of green jubilee.

With laughter riding on the breeze,
The sun gives way to evening's glow,
And all the plants and critters sigh,
As nighttime steals the show!

A Palette of Sunsets

Sky paints its canvas, vibrant and bright,
Maracas shake gently, chasing the night.
Coconuts giggle from palm tree heights,
As sun dips low, sparking silly sights.

Flip-flops flop on sandy shores,
Crabs dance cha-cha, opening doors.
Each wave a whisper of laughter's call,
Seagulls squawk jokes, they're on the ball.

Colors collide in a zany spree,
Like kids in a candy store, wild and free.
The day ends with a splash and a joke,
As fireflies flicker, and spirits stoke.

Giggling stars twinkle above the spree,
Toasting to sunsets, come join me!
With every hue, we wish and beam,
In this palette of laughter, we dare to dream.

Surf and Serenity

Waves tease the shore with a playful grin,
Board shorts flapping like birds in a spin.
Surfboards wobble, splashes abound,
Giggles erupt, like fireworks sound.

A seagull steals chips from a beachside snack,
While a crab plays poker, keeping no track.
Surfing the curls, with friends side by side,
Each tumble and splash fuels laughter's tide.

Sunblock's a battle, slather and swat,
"Just one more layer!" as we laugh a lot.
Sandcastle kings with shells as their crowns,
Decorate their palaces while goofing around.

As twilight lingers, the ocean winks,
Sharing secrets and spontaneous blinks.
With each wave's crash, surprises await,
In this surf and serenity, laughter can't wait.

Pulses of a Golden Dawn

Morning peeks through with wacky delight,
Chasing the snooze, while birds take flight.
Coffee threatens to leap off the pot,
While laughter bubbles, and worries are not.

Sunbeams bounce off the dew-kissed grass,
Making even the grumpiest smile and pass.
Toasters toast bread with a cheeky flair,
As juice spills over—oh, what a scare!

Hats are donning in curious styles,
While squirrels plan heists with cheeky smiles.
The rhythm of day breaks, goofy and bold,
Moments of joy in the sunlight steal gold.

Each tick of the clock is a giggle or two,
In the symphony of dawn, all feels brand new.
With pulses of fun in the morning's embrace,
Life dances wildly in this lively space.

The Tapestry of Rain and Light

Raindrops tap dance on rooftops so sly,
Puddles reflect clouds that drift by.
Umbrellas bloom in styles quite absurd,
As laughter and lightning share a sweet word.

Raincoats parade with colors so bright,
While socks do the cha-cha, a soggy delight.
With splashes that echo like laughter in tune,
Joy's woven together in this whimsical monsoon.

Sunbreaks peep through with a glittering grin,
Painting the world with a mischievous spin.
Rainbows giggle, teasing below,
Hoping for leprechauns, stealing the show.

In this tapestry woven of rain and of light,
Every drop holds a chuckle, dunking with might.
So dance through the puddles, with squeals of delight,
For life's just a party, in this whimsical fight!

Harmony in the Tropics

In the sun, the coconuts sway,
With monkeys who dance and can't delay.
A parrot squawks a tune of cheer,
While lizards perform, without any fear.

Bamboo drinks with muddled zest,
What a thrill, a funny fest!
Flip-flops flapping, seagulls dive,
Nature's comedy, alive and jive.

Palm trees giggle in the breeze,
As the sun sets with playful ease.
The night brings laughter, stars above,
In this paradise, you fall in love.

Coconuts roll and slip around,
With every stumble, joy is found.
Harmony blooms, what a sweet sound,
This merry place, pure magic bound.

The Allure of Hidden Beaches

A beach so fine, it sparkles bright,
Sandy toes, a funny sight.
Hidden gems beneath the sun,
Treasure hunts, oh what fun!

Crabs in costumes, dance with glee,
Waving at you, come play with me!
Shells with stories, all so odd,
Whispers of the ocean, a funny nod.

Fins and laughs, the fish parade,
In a splashy show, they're all displayed.
Salty hair and waves that race,
The beach is home to nature's face!

And as the sunset paints the scene,
Everyone laughs, it's quite routine.
Hidden beaches, full of bliss,
With every wave, you can't miss.

Abundant Hues of Paradise

Colors splash like paint on a wall,
The vibrant hues that enthrall.
From flamingos to the bright blue sky,
Nature puts on a funny tie.

Bananas grin from leafy spots,
While butterflies twirl, tying knots.
A mango sings a juicy tune,
In a fruit salad dance by the moon.

Amidst the greens, a bright peach rare,
Winks at you with a fruity flair.
Laughter erupts from every vine,
As nature jests, calling you to dine.

In paradise, everything's a game,
Even the flowers have their fame!
With colors merry, it feels so right,
A carnival of shades, sheer delight.

The Essence of the Salted Air

Salted breezes tickle the nose,
As seagulls giggle in carefree prose.
Laughter bubbles like a fizzy drink,
Oh, how the seaside makes you think!

Surfboards wobble, here and there,
As surfers tumble without a care.
The waves play tricks, as tides do laugh,
Every splash tells a funny craft.

Windy whispers, tales to share,
Of mischief brewing in the air.
Seashells tell jokes, who knew they could?
In this salty realm, life feels good!

Sunset serenades with colors bold,
Life's salty essence never gets old.
With every breeze comes a hearty cheer,
In a world so lively, nothing to fear.

Secret Whispers of the Sun

The sun peeked out, looking shy,
A speckled grin in the bright blue sky.
Palm trees swayed, singing tunes,
While crabs danced to the beat of loons.

Coconuts dropped with comical thuds,
As seagulls gossiped in merry floods.
Laughter bubbled by the shore,
Where sandcastles grew to heights galore.

The sun sent rays, a ticklish tease,
Causing flip-flops to trip with ease.
Beach balls bounced, oh what a sight,
Chasing shadows in pure delight.

The Spirit of Island Reflections

Mirrors of water, a cheeky grin,
Flopping fish, a splashy win.
Turtles sunbathe, hats askew,
Making selfies as they brew.

The breeze brought jokes from the trees,
Whispered secrets carried with ease.
Bananas laughed upon the vine,
While iguanas sipped on sunshine wine.

Reflections sparkled with sunny glee,
Chasing rainbows, one, two, three.
In the shade, a hammock swayed,
As island dreams danced and played.

Skylines of the Tropics

Kites flew high, a colorful crew,
Swinging left and right, like they knew.
Fruits in hand, a carnival feast,\nWhile bees buzzed tunes,
quite the beast.

Each sunset painted a funny grin,
As crickets chirped, the night to begin.
Stars winked down, mischievous and bright,
Offering advice to the moon's delight.

Palm fronds waved, they'd love a chat,
About the silly habits of a cat.
The skyline glowed with laughter and cheers,
Crafting memories that linger for years.

Dances of Fireflies at Dusk

Fireflies twinkled, a playful show,
Dancing in circles, high and low.
They whispered secrets, soft and bright,
Chasing shadows, a joyous flight.

The breeze played tunes on the grass,
As bunny rabbits hopped with class.
Owls blinked twice, asking for fun,
Joining the party begun by the sun.

With every flutter, a giggle rose,
Like naughty whispers only one knows.
Dusk painted dreams with firefly light,
As laughter echoed through the night.

Coral Castles in the Sun

In vibrant hues, the crabs all play,
Building castles day by day.
With tiny moats of seaweed green,
They cheerfully reign like a sandy queen.

The starfish wear their finest shades,
Waving flags in brilliant glades.
They chuckle loud, they strut with glee,
In this realm as bright as can be.

A parrot squawks a raucous tune,
While dolphins dance beneath the moon.
They park their boats, tell tales of old,
In Coral Castles, magic unfolds.

When sea turtles join the fray,
It's a boisterous, splashing cabaret.
With fishy friends and ocean breeze,
Life is more than just a tease!

Elysium in Bloom

Flowers giggle in sunlit glows,
As bees buzz 'round like tiny pros.
The daisies play tag near the brook,
While tulips nod with a funny look.

Sunflowers wear a silly hat,
Chasing shadows, who's bigger than that?
The garden gnomes, oh what a sight,
Trying to dance, but falling right.

A whimsical breeze tells jokes of old,
As petals tumble, bright and bold.
In this realm where laughter blooms,
The wackiest fun inside each room.

The butterflies join in with flair,
Winging past without a care.
Elysium's laughter fills the skies,
Where joy reigns true, a glorious surprise!

Dance of the Ocean Tides

The waves perform a wobbly jig,
As crabs join in, oh so big!
They tap their pincers, that's the beat,
While seashells clap with happy feet.

Starfish swirl in a lovely spin,
Their graceful moves make the seagulls grin.
With each wave that crashes ashore,
They laugh and play, wanting more.

The fish are twirling in a parade,
In colorful costumes they are displayed.
Splashes erupt as they take flight,
Creating bubbles, a sparkly sight.

The sun dips low, a cheeky glow,
Joining the party, putting on a show.
With ocean tides led by laughter's guide,
It's a festival where fun won't hide!

The Breath of Pineapples

A fruity breeze fills the air,
Pineapples giggle, without a care.
They wear sunglasses, strut around,
In their prickly crowns, they're renowned.

They tell tall tales of sunny lands,
As palm trees sway with open hands.
Through laughter bursts, the scent they share,
Bringing joy as light as air.

Coconuts join with big round grins,
Shaking their shells, as the fun begins.
A party's brewing beneath the sun,
With pineapple punch, oh what a run!

As laughter ripples through the grove,
Sweet scents of fun become the trove.
In this world where laughter is ripe,
A fruity delight, oh what a type!

Soulful Sighs of the Ethereal Isles

Where palm trees dance with giggles bright,
The coconuts wear hats at night.
Seagulls sing their silly song,
While critters prance and all feels wrong.

Bamboo slips on a vibrant shoe,
And waves wave back—oh, what a view!
Laughter echoes through the sand,
As jellyfish join the conga band.

Sunshine tickles the golden shore,
With playful waves that beg for more.
A crab in shades does zany flips,
While island breezes share their quips.

In every nook, a joyful chance,
To make a friend or join the dance.
So raise a drink, let spirits rise,
In this land of giggles and surprise!

Awakening Wild Spirits

The flamingoes flaunt their pink parade,
While monkeys swing in masquerade.
A parrot shrieks, it's party time,
As lizards dance to a funky rhyme.

Coconuts bounce with a cheeky grin,
While turtles practice their grinning spin.
The sun rolls out in a golden coat,
As fish take off in a silly boat.

The breeze blows softly, full of cheer,
As iguanas break into a beer.
With every gust, a giggling sound,
Of wildlife antics all around.

So shake a leg, let loose a shout,
In this land where joy is never out.
Let wild hearts run, let wild tales unfurl,
In a world where chaos can make you twirl!

The Palette of Paradise

Brush strokes splash on skies so blue,
With colors mixed by frogs that coo.
A sunset painted with laughter's glee,
As the sun tosses taffy into the sea.

Crabs in shades play the fashion game,
While the ocean tickles with a teasing name.
A rainbow serpent saunters through,
Splashing paint in every hue.

Bananas giggle when they collide,
With mangoes bouncing like a joyful ride.
In this mad world of art and cheer,
The ferns crack jokes as we draw near.

So dip your toes in vibrant fun,
While kooky dreams are spun like sun.
This canvas teems with sweet delight,
Where every brush is a silly sight!

Mirth in the Melodic Rain

Raindrops tap dance on the leaves,
Creating jokes that nature weaves.
A frog in slippers leaps with glee,
While fish dance disco under the sea.

Umbrellas pop open, bright and bold,
As laughter mingles with tales retold.
The clouds play tag in the sky up high,
While snacks rain down as sprightly pie.

Singing showers sing a tune,
As puddles giggle beneath the moon.
Glorious droplets, a splash of fun,
With every drop, giggles run.

So twirl and whirl in the playful storm,
As laughter's bubbles begin to swarm.
Embrace the joy, let hearts refrain,
For mirth awakes in the melodic rain!

Vibrations of Celestial Flora

In the jungle, where vines twist and sway,
The flowers giggle, come out to play.
A parrot jokes with a friendly bee,
Their laughter echoes, wild and free.

A monkey swings, doing cartwheels neat,
While sloths take naps, oh, can't be beat!
The trees shake hands with the breeze so bright,
As sunbeams dance in morning light.

The orchids wink under moonlight's kiss,
And frogs croak tunes that you can't miss.
With every rustle, the night gets loud,
Nature's jesters, a lively crowd.

So sip your juice from a coconut bowl,
And join the party where the wild things roll.
Let the flora tickle your funny bone,
In this paradise, you're never alone.

Hidden Treasures of the Cove

At the shore where the secrets softly hide,
Shells tell tales of the fish who glide.
Crabs in tuxedos march with flair,
While the seaweed dances without a care.

A treasure map made of bright sea glass,
Leads to a picnic where good times amass.
The gulls drop hints while they take a dive,
For the best-hidden snacks that you'll contrive.

In the cove, the legend comes alive,
With octopuses ready to high-five.
The starfish spin in their vibrant coats,
As a dolphin hums while it happily floats.

Come share the giggles and sandcastle feats,
Where laughter's the spice in our beachy treats.
Between the waves, let your worries wash,
And relish the joy in our seaside posh.

Enchantment by the Lagoon

Beneath the palms, where the water gleams,
The frogs croon softly, lost in dreams.
A dragonfly prances, a nature show,
While fish jump up for a splashy throw.

The banter of reeds whispers in the air,
As turtles pull faces without a care.
A heron practices its runway walk,
While crickets gather for a late-night talk.

In the moonlight's glow, the lilies sway,
As fireflies twinkle in a dazzling display.
The lagoon's charm brings giggles anew,
With every ripple, a joke or two.

So join the merriment, do not delay,
In this enchanted spot where we laugh and play.
With each soft wave, let your spirit roam,
In the cozy laughter, you'll find your home.

Under the Canopy's Spell

Under branches, a wacky parade,
Where critters concoct a grand charade.
The raccoons wear hats, looking so chic,
While laughter bursts from a wise old leak.

Squirrels gossip near the old oak tree,
Their chatter so loud, it's hard to foresee.
A bunch of owls hoot a catchy song,
Feathers all ruffled, they can't go wrong.

Behold the magic of shadows and light,
Where every nook is a giggle delight.
Imaginary friends leap and bound,
In a world so wacky, laughter is found.

So join the fun under nature's veil,
Where every whisper is a comical tale.
Together we'll wander, let spirits excel,
Lost in the wonder of the canopy's spell.

The Color Wheel of Water

The sea wore shades of turquoise flair,
Rubber ducks sailed without a care.
The sun donned a bright orange hat,
While crabs danced like they were at a mat.

Green seaweed waved, beckoning to play,
A fish wore sunglasses, oh what a day!
With a splash and a giggle, joy took flight,
Even the dolphins joined in the delight.

Bubbles rose like laughter in the air,
And starfish cheered from their sandy lair.
The coral reefs threw a color parade,
A wiggly noodle, mischief displayed.

With each wave's boast, the colors confound,
In this vibrant ocean where silliness is found.
The tide ticks away like a cheeky watch,
Let's paint the waves, who needs a swatch!

Shoreline Symphony

Crabs conducting with their little claws,
A concert of waves, applause with a pause.
The seagulls chimed in with a squawky tune,
While shells collected serenades for noon.

The wind played piano, soft and sweet,
As sandcastles crumbled beneath tiny feet.
Each child laughed like a trumpet's blare,
Building dreams in castles, full of flair.

Starfish spun like ballerinas in the sun,
And seashells whispered, 'Oh, this is fun!'
The ocean's rhythm danced through the air,
A symphony created with joy to spare.

So grab your flip-flops, join the grand spree,
For life's a joke sung by waves and glee.
Each splash is a giggle, each tide a cheer,
The shoreline's a stage, come join, lend your ear!

Beneath the Leaping Moon

The moon jumped high, a bouncing balloon,
While fish played tag in a watery tune.
Stars twinkled like lights in a silly parade,
As jellyfish wiggled in a shimmering charade.

A crab in a tuxedo strutted with pride,
While sea turtles danced with grace on the tide.
The night chuckled softly, a giggly breeze,
As waves told secrets to the swaying trees.

With shadows that twirled, mischief at play,
Mermaids laughed loud in their Undersea Café.
Each splash was a chuckle, the sea painted bright,
In this comedic ballet, the world felt just right.

So join the frolic under the moon's glow,
With fishy whispers, let the laughter flow.
For here in the dark, with a wink and a grin,
The ocean's a stage where the fun will begin!

Emissaries of the Indian Ocean

The fish wore hats as they swam with flair,
A flamboyant parade of aquatic players.
Whales joked around with a melodious splash,
While octopuses twirled, creating a splash.

A parrot squawked secrets from above,
As dolphins hip-hopped in a dance of love.
The ocean's antics, a sight to behold,
Stories of silliness, cheerfully told.

Starfish sent postcards from sandy retreats,
While crabs shared snacks in their cozy suites.
They waved at the moon in a goofy salute,
Pledging mischief by day, and at night, to hoot.

The currents chuckled, breezy with fun,
In this Indian realm where laughter's begun.
So come ride the waves, join the unruly band,
For here, at the beach, life's delightfully grand!

A Symphony of Mangroves

In a swampy stage where the critters play,
The crabs dance like they're at a cabaret.
With each splash and croak, they form a tune,
While the heron orders dinner at high noon.

Mosquitoes join in with a buzzing band,
While the frogs clap in a soft, wet land.
The mangroves sway like they just don't care,
As a parrot squawks jokes for folks passing there.

Jellyfish float like balloons on a string,
As the dolphins toss seaweed like it's a fling.
The pelicans mime in a silly parade,
Where the ocean's laughter can never fade.

Even the fish play a game of charades,
Making sure no one forgets the escapades.
Together they join in the wacky delight,
In the mangrove's embrace, from morning to night.

The Rhythm of Ocean Breezes

The wind whispers secrets that tickle the shore,
It steals hats from heads and just begs for more.
Sandy toes wiggle with every gust's kiss,
As laughter erupts over a tasty fish dish.

Seagulls are crooning a tune on their flight,
Expecting applause from shells dressed up bright.
In the distance, a surfer attempts a new dance,
Only to tumble, not giving up his chance.

Palm trees twist in their own funny fashion,
While beach balls bounce with ungracious passion.
The sun, with a wink, juggles rays of gold,
While children squeal with their ice creams untold.

A crab in a bow tie struts on the sand,
Declaring himself the king of this land.
The rhythm of breezes will make you giggle,
As the ocean's embrace keeps the laughter a wiggle.

Lush Canopy's Embrace

Beneath the green veil, the creatures convene,
Where the monkeys swing like they're on a trampoline.
Parrots wear fancy outfits and gossip away,
While the sloth takes a selfie—what a display!

In shadows where sunshine just peeks out to play,
The vines do the cha-cha in a comical sway.
With every bright leaf, there's a tickling sound,
As nature's comedians gather around.

The rain joins the fun with a pitter-pat beat,
While frogs in tuxedos dance close to your feet.
A snail, with his bling, struts down slow and grand,
Leaving the others to think he's in demand.

The jests of the jungle are never quite done,
As the sun peeks through to say, "Let's have some fun!"
In the lush canopy's embrace, joyfully bright,
Life's a joke where the giggles take flight.

Awakening the Coral Heart

Beneath the waves, where the colors collide,
The fish throw a bash, holding nothing inside.
An octopus juggles while seahorses cheer,
As the coral reef joins the bubbly frontier!

With a wink and a swirl, the clownfish take stage,
Their antics and colors are all the rage.
A snail gets a laugh with his hard shelled race,
While the starfish stretch out in a luxurious space.

The seaweed sways like a dancer in trance,
While a turtle attempts to perfect his prance.
The coral heart beats in vibrant delight,
As the underwater world giggles with might.

The sunbeams filter through in a shimmering show,
Where laughter and bubbles effortlessly flow.
In this joyful ocean, where peculiar things start,
Nature's humor thrives, awakening the heart.

Whispered Promises of the Jungle

In the jungle, where the monkeys swing,
A parrot steals my breakfast, the cheeky thing.
Lemurs laugh in the trees, quite a sight,
As I trip over roots, oh what a fright!

Bamboo shakes in the breeze with a sound,
As sloths move slowly, barely off the ground.
Coconut falls like a playful soft tap,
While I dodge it—oops! Now that's a mishap!

Butterflies giggle as they flutter on by,
Creating a crown for the queen bee who'll fly.
Frogs croak in chorus, a most lively song,
In this jungle of wonders, where all feels wrong!

We dance 'round the trees, all wild and free,
Where the laughter of critters makes us all glee.
With whispers and promises beneath the green,
Who knew a jungle could be this serene?

Colors Unfurled at Dawn

Morning comes, with a burst of bright hue,
Chickens roll out, clucking, not knowing what to do.
The sun paints the sky, a canvas so wide,
While I trip over crayons that rolled from their side!

Mangoes tumble down, ripe and round,
Ducks dive for breakfast, splash all around.
A toucan insists on acting quite rude,
With a beak like a clown, it's causing a feud!

The palm leaves swish, tickling my nose,
As I dance through the garden in mismatched clothes.
Laughter erupts from the hibiscus bloom,
As I twirl, and tumble and sail past the room!

The day wakes with colors, oh what a sight,
Even the crabs scuttle left and right.
In this joyful ballet beneath the warm sky,
Who knew waking up could make birds fly high!

Echoes of the Bountiful Isles

On the shores of laughter, where the coconuts roll,
A crab pinches my toe, oh what a stroll!
Seagulls squawk tales of their grand ocean flight,
While I chase my own shadow, oh what a sight!

The waves clap their hands, a rhythm so fun,
While I wiggle my toes in the sand, just begun.
Papayas grin widely under the sun's glare,
As the breeze tells secrets, blowing through my hair!

A parrot bursts forth with gossip most sly,
About the pelican's plunge and the fish that fly.
Bigger than dreams, with stories to tell,
As I giggle and gawk at the tide's mighty swell!

Islands dance gaily with butterflies bright,
Where laughter and nature collide with delight.
In this echoing paradise, life feels like play,
With each salty splash, I cheer through the day!

The First Light on Dappled Paths

With the first light, the critters emerge,
A raccoon steals snacks, oh what a surge!
Squirrels recruit, their army is strong,
While the shadows play tricks and all feel wrong.

Beneath the trees, where daffodils sway,
A quirky old turtle leads the ballet.
The carpet of leaves, a crunchy delight,
As I skip down the path, laughter takes flight!

The sun sneaks through branches, a spotlight so bright,
Bouncing off ferns, igniting pure light.
Chirps fill the air, in a comical tune,
As we giggle along with the moon's déjà vu!

Footprints of fun, in the soft morning dew,
Every step echoes, as if saying, "who?"
With a wink and a grin, my heart's full of cheer,
In this joyful beginning, the world feels sincere!

Rebirth under the Mango Tree

In the shade of a mango, I swing and I sway,
Dreaming of pirates on a bright sunny day.
The mangoes are dancing, their sweet little jig,
While I'm finding humor in that silly twig.

I spotted a squirrel with a nut in his mouth,
He slipped on a branch, headed straight for the south.
The mangoes are laughing, all plump and all round,
As the squirrel heads back up, he's so silly and bound.

Banana leaves chuckle, they shake in the breeze,
Throwing shade at the sun as I rest at my ease.
The birds make their gossip in chirps and in tweets,
While I'm munching a mango, life's fresh, oh so sweet.

The breeze has its stories, as shows off its flair,
Even the ants join in, scurrying with care.
Underneath the mango, life swirls and it spins,
Stories wrapped in laughter, where the joy never ends.

Songs of the Ocean Breeze

The ocean sings softly, a lullaby tune,
While crabs do a dance under the bright silver moon.
The dolphins are laughing, leaping with glee,
As they splash my poor toes, what a humorous spree!

Seagulls are squawking, they argue and fight,
Over a chip on the sand, what a comical sight.
The waves roll their eyes, with a foamy good cheer,
As I shake off the water, then someone yells, "Deer!"

Shells spin like records, beneath feathered feet,
Every twist of their rhythm brings laughter so sweet.
Pirates of mischief, they sail from the shore,
Chasing giggles and hiccups, they always want more.

The ocean waves beckon, come dance with the breeze,
As I join the shenanigans, life's joy like the seas.
In this silly embrace, with the sun's happy glow,
Every laugh sends a ripple, as time starts to flow.

Blossoms of the Morning Tide

The flowers awaken with a giggle and yawn,
In the daylight that spills with the rise of the dawn.
Petals are painting their stories in hues,
As bees buzz around like they're out for a cruise.

Dewdrops sparkle, they twinkle like eyes,
While butterflies flutter, making soft, silly sighs.
"Where's the nectar?" they tease, in whimsical flight,
As they prance on the petals, oh, what a sight!

The tulips are gossiping, "Look at that bee!"
"His dance moves are wild, can he please let it be?"
The daisies join in, with a chuckle or two,
As they toss their white heads, like, "What's a bee to do?"

Morning brings laughter, in this garden of glee,
Every bloom's got a story, just waiting for me.
With flowers conversing, and nature's parade,
The joy in the petals, the sweetest charade.

Captured by the Wildflowers

In fields where wildflowers throw colorful spritz,
I tripped on a daisies, oh, nature's great wit!
They giggled and swayed, as I found my way down,
While butterflies joined in, spreading joy all around.

The poppies are whispering, secrets so bold,
While dandelions chuckle, as stories unfold.
A bee crossed my path, wearing pollen like bling,
In the dance of the flowers, life's a joyous fling!

Honeybees battle with ladybugs too,
"Who's the best dancer?" They can't seem to view.
With petals a-twitchin', and bugs in a trance,
Every swirl of the breeze leads to a goofball romance.

Captured by laughter, in hues soft and bright,
In the arms of the wildflowers, everything's right.
With colors and giggles, the day starts with flair,
In this kooky dance, life's laughter we share.

Nature's Revival in Bloom

In gardens where the colors burst,
A snail's parade leads, oh so cursed.
The flowers giggle, swaying free,
As bees buzz by for a cup of tea.

The sunbeam tickles, oh what a tease,
While ants march on with perfect ease.
A fruit falls down with comical flair,
The raccoon shrugs, without a care.

A plump lime rolls, slips on the ground,
A giggling frog leaps, no one around.
While butterflies dance in funny pairs,
Nature's jest is found everywhere.

So take a breath and join the spree,
For blooms are laughing joyfully.
With all the quirks the wild can show,
Nature's punchline puts on a show.

Moments in the Coconut Grove

Coconuts tumble in a cheeky race,
As goats dance 'round with a silly grace.
The palms do sway with a playful cheer,
And vulture giggles, so loud and clear.

A crab in shades struts down the sand,
While lizards groove, oh isn't it grand?
The ocean laughs with foamy glee,
As kids splash high, falling with glee.

In the hammock, a sloth's snooze is bold,
He dreams of dances from days of old.
The breeze brings scents of piña colada,
And dolphins jump – it's a real balada!

Amidst the fun, the sun dips low,
Silly moments put on a show.
So grab your drink, let worries go,
In coconut wonders, laughter will flow.

Rhythms of the Sun-Kissed Earth

The rooster crows like it's on a stage,
With a hat made of leaves, oh what a rage.
The mangoes giggle, ripe and round,
As squirrels wobble without a sound.

Sunshine prances on the joyous lane,
Where turtles race with a bit of disdain.
The chorus of frogs croaks quite off-key,
Yet every note is pure harmony.

The grasshoppers play their stringed tunes,
While crickets band under the moons.
A flower sneezes, sending petals adrift,
Nature's concert, a lovely gift.

Dance with the winds, let laughter resound,
In this cheery place, joy can be found.
With rhythms alive, the heart takes flight,
Sun-kissed magic makes every day bright.

Fragrant Resurgence of the Rainforest

In the rainforest, laughter breaks free,
As monkeys swing on vines, filled with glee.
The orchids yawn, stretching wide,
While sloths opt for a lazy slide.

A parrot squawks, fashionably late,
In a beak full of fruit, oh what a state!
The river gurgles a bubbly tune,
While fireflies dance beneath the moon.

The cocoa beans whisper secrets sweet,
A punchline lands with each little beat.
With every rustle, the forest grins,
In this fragrant jungle, everyone wins.

So come along, join in the fun,
Under the canopy, we all run.
With jokes in the flora, oh so divine,
The rainforest revels in humor's twine.

Nature's Renaissance in Green

In a land where coconuts grin,
The parrots plot mischief within.
Palm trees dance in their leafy best,
As crabs break into a silly jest.

Lizards wear sunglasses in style,
While monkeys swing with cheeky guile.
The flowers bloom with snickers and cheer,
As frogs croak jokes you can barely hear.

The sun shines bright on this joking spree,
As iguanas bask, happy and free.
With each twist of vine and giggle,
Nature laughs—it's a raucous wiggle!

Butterflies flutter, spreading cheer,
With a wink, they disappear.
A renaissance of giggles in green,
In this wild world, oh what a scene!

Mysteries of the Coral Cove

Under waves where fish wear socks,
Clownfish play in polka-dot blocks.
Turtles bob in shades of blue,
While octopuses juggle—who knew?

In a cove of secrets, a shrimp throws a dance,
While sea urchins boast of their spiky romance.
Starfish sit pondering life's great quest,
While dolphins giggle—who's the best jest?

The corals giggle in colors so bright,
As sea cucumbers slip out of sight.
With a splash of humor, the ocean's alive,
In every crevice, the laughter will thrive!

So dive deep and hear what they say,
The mysteries of the cove at play.
With humor beneath the waves, we find,
A world that giggles, wonderfully unconfined!

Island Reverie

On sandy shores where flip-flops roam,
Seagulls steal fries, calling it 'home'.
Beach balls bounce with boisterous delight,
While crabs in tuxedos begin their flight.

Palm trees whisper secrets so sweet,
As sunburnt tourists shuffle their feet.
The waves sing tunes of whimsical glee,
While sunscreen fights a losing decree.

Shells giggle as they tell of the tide,
With starfish as actors, the ocean's pride.
A hammock sways with a contented sigh,
While a lazy lizard plots, "Should I fly?"

With every laugh from the island's heart,
Life's a puzzle, a rascally art.
In this sandy retreat, we find our groove,
An island reverie that makes us move!

Dawn Over Emerald Shores

As dawn breaks with a cheeky grin,
Coconuts wobble, ready to spin.
The roosters crow in a comical way,
While flamingos begin their ballet display.

The waves laugh softly, teasing the sand,
As hibiscus flowers strike a pose, so grand.
The sun peeks over in golden attire,
While geckos toast with drinks of desire.

Children giggle with shells in hand,
Building castles that will not withstand.
Crabs join in, with a marching band,
As laughter echoes across the strand.

Dawn over shores that play and tease,
Brings smiles and giggles with each gentle breeze.
In this merry moment, let worries soar,
As fun unfolds on this vibrant shore!

Tropical Serenade

Coconuts grin with a smile,
Sipping juice, let's stay awhile.
Parrots squawk in stylish flair,
Join the party, if you dare!

Sunshine bounces on the floor,
Crabs are dancing, who could ask for more?
Bikini-clad, the beach folks cheer,
Sandy toes are the best souvenir!

Flip-flops flop, a playful sound,
While ukuleles twang around.
Surfboards line the vibrant bay,
Catch a wave or just play today!

As the sun dips, the stars appear,
Tiki lights blink, let's give a cheer!
Laughter echoes, all feels right,
In this paradise of sheer delight!

Dance of the Hibiscus

In a garden full of bloom,
Hibiscus twirls, dispelling gloom.
Bees are buzzing, doing the jig,
While I attempt a hula gig!

Lizards leap with cheeky flair,
Trying to catch me unaware.
Each flower boasts a vibrant hue,
As if they want to join the crew!

Honey dripping from a pine,
Crackers crunched, it's snack time!
Balloons float above the ground,
Whimsical giggles all around!

When the sun sets and the moon takes flight,
We dance till dawn, under stars so bright.
With every sway, and every laugh,
Nature leads, it's a perfect path!

Swaying in the Warmth

Palm trees sway like dancing hands,
Excited whispers fill the sands.
Sunglasses perched with perfect ease,
Watch the ants throw a wild tease!

Fruits roll by like bowling balls,
Mangoes laughing at tropical calls.
Sun hats tip, and coolers crack,
While sunscreen glows on my back!

Meeting friends like seagulls squawking,
Sharing tales while the waves are talking.
With silly hats and goofy grins,
Who knew fun could bring such wins?

Even the breeze giggles in delight,
While hammock naps become a sight.
So let's toast to this lively spree,
In our sun-kissed, wild jubilee!

Morning Mist Beneath the Coconut Trees

Misty mornings with lazy vibes,
Coconut secrets that each tree scribes.
Roosters crow, they're out of tune,
While I chase my mango smoothie soon!

Underneath the leafy shade,
Crickets cradle their serenade.
Bongo beats and laughter flow,
What a show the critters know!

Fog lifting like a curtain's tease,
I've found a dance while sipping bees.
Swaying limbs and rustling leaves,
Nature's humor never deceives!

As the sun breaks, the day begins,
With laughter tangled in our spins.
Here's to mornings made of zest,
Where silly joy is always best!

Fables of the Beach

In flip-flops made of jelly, they parade,
Crabs in shades, a fashion crusade.
Seagulls gossip in a squawky tone,
While sunburnt tourists claim the throne.

Palm trees sway, like they're in a trance,
As beach balls jiggle, chaos in dance.
Sandcastles rise, with moats of fun,
But watch out! Here comes a splash and a run.

Chasing after a runaway hat,
The dog steals it, oh, imagine that!
With a bark and leap, he claims his prize,
Leaving laughter and sunlit skies.

Ice cream drips down a melted cone,
Bees join the party, buzzing their own.
It's a fable, yes, but oh so real,
Life at the beach, a whimsical wheel.

Awakening Sweet Scents

Pineapple teasing with a grin so sweet,
Mangoes dancing, a juicy treat.
Coconuts giggle from high above,
As laughter fills the air, full of love.

The barbecue sizzles with a meaty cheer,
Friends gather 'round, bringing good beer.
Each bite savored, a flavor parade,
In this feast of joy, no need to evade.

Sandy toes and sticky fingers galore,
Somebody's lost a flip-flop—oh, what a chore!
A piña colada spills with a splash,
But giggles explode—a hilarious crash!

The scent of sunscreen, a funny perfume,
Mixes with laughter that fills every room.
In this paradise, under the sun's rays,
The sweetest of moments fill our days.

Kaleidoscope of Island Delights

Colors shimmer like a rainbow's kiss,
Bananas in hats, pure island bliss.
Papaya sings with a fruity zest,
While pineapples woo, they're dressed in their best.

Sunsets that giggle, paint the sky,
While fireflies wink, oh my, oh my!
Twirling tiki torches light up the night,
As laughter erupts under stars shining bright.

Waves play peek-a-boo, splashing about,
The sand ticks tickle as kids jump and shout.
Kites soar high, painted like dreams,
In this kaleidoscope, nothing's as it seems.

Every grin forged in salt and in play,
Stories spun under the sun's golden ray.
Island delights, a canvas so wide,
Where joy paints the heart, in laughter we glide.

Laughter Among the Waves

Waves whisper secrets, tickling the shore,
Shells collecting giggles, who could ask for more?
Splash fights erupt with squeals and shrieks,
As gulls chirp tales, their beaks full of peaks.

A beach ball bounces into a picnic spread,
Sandwiches fly, who's hungry? Nobody's fed!
Kites tangled up in a feathery mess,
The winds are laughing, I must confess.

Surfers ride waves like a merry-go-round,
With a big splash, they vanish, no one around.
Floating on laughter, the day melts away,
Every tickle of sea salt leads us to play.

A sunburned lobster shrieks in delight,
As flip-flops dance in a comedic plight.
Among the waves, our worries all cease,
In this ocean of fun, we find our peace.

Serenade of the Palm Fronds

In the breeze, palms dance like cats,
Swinging low, wearing tiny hats.
Coconuts drop with a thud and a bounce,
Squirrels scamper, filled with their flounce.

Fronds whisper secrets they'd never tell,
About the iguana who tripped and fell.
Parrots squawk, 'What a clumsy sight!'
Echoing laughter in morning light.

Beneath the shade where shadows play,
A toucan snacks on a bright papaya.
He mischievously drops it on a frog,
Who croaks and jumps like a silly hog.

With every rustle, the whole scene's a show,
In this quirky land, where the sun's glow.
Palm fronds serenade with a funny twist,
Nature's humor, you can't resist!

Awakening in the Canopy

Up high in branches, monkeys swing,
Wearing smiles, oh what joy they bring!
They giggle and hiss, with sass and flair,
    Throwing fruit as if they care.

The toucan's beak shines bright, oh dear,
He trips on a vine while sipping beer.
Parrots chuckle, 'What a silly show!'
    As they mimic him, in a row.

Sunlight filters through leaves, a glowing tease,
    Awakens the sloth, oh what a breeze!
He yawns and stretches, but stays right there,
    Laziness is his favorite affair.

In this buzzing world, where quirks collide,
    Laughter erupts with each fun ride.
    Canopy life, a comedic spree,
    Bringing smiles from tree to tree!

Colors of the Rising Horizon

As dawn breaks with a splash of hue,
The flamingos gossip in shades of blue.
Jellyfish float while turtles glide,
Even the sand crabs take a bold stride.

Golden rays warm up the beach and sea,
While seagulls compete for the biggest freebie.
They squawk and swoop, causing a rift,
Stealing snacks like it's their best gift.

The horizon blushes, a canvas so bright,
As dolphins leap, putting on a nightlight.
A whale waves close with a splash and a grin,
"Mornings like these make my heart spin!"

In this patch of bliss where colors collide,
Every wacky moment is a joyride.
Nature painted laughter across the sky,
With each brush stroke, just ask why!

Horizon's Breath

The sun yawns wide, stretching its rays,
Waking the world in comical ways.
Dancing waves with playful bites,
Crabs boogie in their sandy tights.

Breezes pirouette around the shore,
Tickling the toes, begging for more.
A parrot shouts, 'Catch me, if you dare!'
While a hermit crab finds its mismatched chair.

In the laughter of waves, sea otters play,
Sliding and tumbling in a foamy ballet.
Fish flip up high, "Look at me shine!"
Making bubbles that tickle the spine.

Amidst this chaos, joy's in the air,
Each moment's a treasure, whimsical flair.
Horizon's laughter, a merry affair,
Breathing fun into the warm, salty air!

The Soul of Sunlit Waters

In the pool of laughter, fish swim by,
With sun hats on, looking sly.
Crabs doing cha-cha on the sandy shore,
As seagulls giggle, asking for more.

Mermaids in shells, they hold a sale,
Selling dreams caught in a seaweed tail.
Rubber duckies parade in a line,
While octopuses dance and sip on brine.

The beach ball bounces, a laugh in the air,
Sunburned tourists with sandy hair.
Coconuts wink, they're quite the jest,
In a world where fun is the honored quest.

Watermelons float, wearing shades of blue,
While jellyfish tease with a wink or two.
Everything giggles under the sun's ray,
In the water, where joy comes out to play.

Kisses from the Sea Breeze

The wind whispers secrets with a playful laugh,
As beach towels fly by, like sails on a craft.
Flip-flops are dancing, lost in the fun,
While crabs throw a party, all on the run.

Salty air tickles and makes us sneeze,
Caught in the charm of the teasing breeze.
Seashells gossip, they're quite the swells,
Reciting tales of their oceanic spells.

Pineapple hats nod, giving sweet cheer,
As surfboards join in, they're quite the dear.
Laughter erupts, like bubbles on foam,
In this place where every wave feels like home.

With splashes of joy, the shore sings delight,
Balloons floating high, a colorful sight.
The sea offers kisses, a soft little breeze,
And life is a party as wild as you please.

Heartbeat of the Jungle

The vines are giggling, they twirl and tease,
While monkeys swing by with acrobatic ease.
Parrots in bowties, they squawk with delight,
As lizards breakdance under the moonlight.

In the wild, the beats are funny and bright,
Where hippos wear shades and dance through the night.
Frogs serenade stars with a croaky croon,
Imitating saxophones under the moon.

Bamboo flutes play serenades to the trees,
While squirrels throw nuts, as if to appease.
The jungle's a party, with rhythms so free,
Where nature laughs loud, just come and see.

Sloths take their time, they play it so slow,
While chattering toucans steal the whole show.
In this vibrant jungle, joy never hides,
With the heartbeat of laughter that swells and glides.

Blossoms in the Morning Light

Dewdrops giggle on petals so bright,
While flowers gossip in morning's soft light.
Bees wear tiny hats, buzzing with fun,
As butterflies dance, their colors outrun.

The sun winks down with a playful tone,
Making shadows laugh, they're never alone.
Budding blooms chuckle, as if in a race,
To see who can bloom with the funniest face.

A garden of joys, each blossom a cheer,
Tickling the sky, as it bends to hear.
With flowers in hula-hoops, having a ball,
In a merry parade, there's joy for us all!

Petunias pout and daisies, they sway,
As the morning giggles, leading the way.
With a wink from the sun, and a joyful sight,
The world bursts forth in blossomed delight.